Plethora Of Poems

A New Dawn

_— of —_

A Hundred Hues

MONICA PREM BAJAJ

First Published in September 2021

ISBN: 978-93-5427-840-2

BLUEROSE PUBLISHERS
www.bluerosepublishers.com
info@bluerosepublishers.com
+91 8882 898 898

Cover Design:
Palak

Cover Page Art:
Leonida Arte, Novi Sad, Europe

Typographic Design:
Namrata Saini

Distributed by: BlueRose, Amazon, Flipkart, Shopclues

❖ *Main aim of any poem is to thrill its readers and vibrate. Poems by Monica have succeeded in exactly achieving that goal. Being a longtime poetry reader in Twitter, I have found her to be both - a brilliant Poetess and an ideal human being.*
Wishing Monica more and more success!
Deepak Kanungo
Editor, Odia Encyclopedia
Bhubaneswar.
Email @53dkbk@gmail.com.

❖ *Writing of what cannot be supposed or controlled, Monica weaves words of love and loss, with colorful imagination and stunning originality. Captivating soulful stirrings presented in ways that shatter algorithms while capturing my heart, I allow Monica's words to wander deep within, touching internal spots previously bereft of feeling... with love, happiness and all the longing I hadn't known I was missing.*
Richard Baron DeRosa
Pl Beach, Florida

❖ *Monica is wandering among the words*
As if she is in a garden of flowers
The words bloom with her soft touches
And volunteer to give her their best essences
She uses the essences to make the best honey
which we can call it exquisite poetry
Khan Eagle
Poet
Turkey

❖ *It is rare to find a poet that can ignite the imagination, raise emotions and lead the reader along a journey. Monica is one of those rare and gifted poets that does just these things. A kind person and a talented writer; her poems are an intimate gift she shares so graciously. Proud to call Monica a friend, and happy to celebrate her poetry! Enjoy the reading experience!*
Michael Valentine
Master Certified Counsellor
New York ,USA

❖ *Monica's poetry comes from a place where nature and love meet in secret and blossom into amazing beauty. Her words are a celebration of living, and I stop and read every one of them, confidant they guide the footsteps of my heart on the safest journey.*
Christopher Mahan
Software Engineer & Writer
Los Angeles, USA

❖ *Monica is a poetess of deep emotions, who reveals her soul, Painting her world with beautiful and graceful pictures of sublime thoughts, playing with ornaments of the words …Where clouds cradle dreams. Poems lead the reader directly to the heart. In the weaving of her poetry, we can feel the beats of love. Monica represents every woman in the waves of life, love, longing, passion, searching for hope, announcing the arrival of a new dawn in a hundreds of hues.*
Leonida Arte
International Artist & Architect
Novi Sad, Europe

❖ *A few times in life, you come across people who you immediately trust unconditionally. Monica is one of them. I've trust in her and her writings.*
Scott Maarten Hefti
Photographer & Anthropologist
Netherlands

❖ *Monica is a poet who writes from her heart, each poem is a gift, you feel every word. As if she's speaking straight to your soul, by weaving a special magic with her art. A kind heart, a dear friend and an amazing poet; she is a must read.*
Maureen O'Dea
Poet & Artist
USA

❖ *Monica's poems always express & touch the depths of Soulful yearnings & breath-taking, delightful inspirations. Sometimes raw, dark, sensuous, earthy. Sometimes exquisitely delicate, light as a feather ascending heights of Spirit. Always woven together with brilliant use of language.*
Leslie Tylersmith
Practitioner Of Healing Arts
Brooklyn, NY, USA

❖ *It's a splendid feeling to see my creation as a header page with great poems. It is a terrific surprise to read Monica's excellent poetry. Monica, wish you amazing success!*
Donna Marie Hamer
Calgary Alberta Canada

❖ *Monica is so kind heart and the way she writes is so inspiring ..the way she sews the words with each other, merging them to make beautiful sensible poems and the way she uses the most rare words sometimes putting it to express her feelings. Monica writes about each and every topic with ultimate passion ...the way she speaks about love is the way of her heart how it floats to reach the heaven making us fly to the sky .I can touch the clouds with her talent which is a symphony to make every feelings in a harmony. She writes songs in our hearts. She starts with love and her words has no ends and above all, she is an angel of poetesses. She is a blessing.*
Sema Küçük
Poet
Türkiye /İstanbul /Bayrampaşa

Plethora Of Poems

A New Dawn

— of —

A Hundred Hues

MONICA PREM BAJAJ

Dedicated

To the
Most affable
And
Absolutely essential person
The Benign Reader
Who inculcated a desire to
Get my words printed

To my parents & Brother, Aditya
Who taught me
How to hold on
To a dream

To My Loving husband, Prem Bajaj
For his unending patience with me

To my Earth Angels-
My daughters,
Kritagya & Devagya
For realizing me that
My spirit is stronger than my fears.

Acknowledgments

Writing my first book has been both challenging and invigorating and I couldn't have done it alone. With the deepest gratitude I wish to express my thanks to every person who inspired, touched, and illuminated my life through their presence. I'm deeply indebted to my indomitable editor, Dr Linda M Best, USA, for her genuine apprehensions, guidance and confidence in my ability to get this done. I would like to acknowledge and express my immense gratitude to-

- » Leonida Arte, Novi Sad, Europe, for her painting 'Touch Of Heaven' for Cover Page.
- » Priya Kushwaha, India, for her painting 'Serenity' for Part-1 Header Page and stunning illustrations.
- » Scott Maarten Hefti, Netherlands, for his photograph 'Simplicity' for Part-2 Header Page.
- » Maureen O'Dea, USA, for her painting 'How Do I Love Thee' for Part-3 Header Page.
- » Donna Marie Hamer, Australia, for her painting 'Purple Flowers' for Part-4 Header Page.
- » Leslie Tylersmith, USA, for her painting 'Journey Into Heart Of Light' for Part-5 Header Page.
- » Bela, India, for her Icon design.
- » Paritosh, India, for his encouragement & exceptional support.

Synopsis

My life has always been on a rollercoaster ride indulging in inevitable experiences of pleasure and pain in juxtaposition. When life's challenges became overwhelming I started searching myself in words that gave me wisdom to realise that darkness does not diminish light. The heart's desire to build its own world brings forth my unexplored region of existence in the shape of 'A New Dawn Of A Hundred Hues'

Each poem in this book , 'A New Dawn Of A Hundred Hues' will touch your heartstrings, speak to your spirits and enhance your consciousness. This plethora of poems is divided into five sections. Each section is composed of poems that demonstrates the concept of categories. The first part, 'Nature's Rendezvous With Reveries' is enhanced by natural beauty and sing melodies of the divine gifts of God to human beings. The second part, 'The Glory Of Stillness' emphasizes the relevance of solitude and stillness. These poems carry dark with streaks of light. The third part , 'Let Me Love Thee' comprises the poems of love and desires. Here, love occupies the status of Deity. The fourth part, 'Lilac Shades Of Life' depicts the various hues of life that will leave the reader exploring asserting, questioning and probing its new vistas. The fifth part, 'Musings Of My Soul' gives glimpses of our intricate, intuitive, and magnificent soul. These poems take you to the innermost beauty of self at deeper level where fragments of our souls are scattered.

As you travel through its pages, you'll feel a personal connection because ' A New Dawn Of A Hundred Hues' has been created for you. May the experience of reading this book leave you in a sense of delight, awe and wonder!

I've made butterflies of words

To spread joys in void arcane

I give all I have in me

For you, I've beautified my pain

Table Of Contents

Part-2
Glory Of Stillness

Part- 3
Let Me Love Thee

Part- 5
Musings Of My Soul

Part - 1
Nature's Rendezvous With
Reveries

Morning Hymn

Moon took the last yawn
Announced the arrival of dawn
Birds unlock their throats
Sunflowers giggle and sunrays float
She dresses herself in fabric benign
Her morning hymn to heaven sublime

Grand Arch Of The Sky

Grand arch bridges the way from earth to the sky
How gloriously the colourful bow crossing
Over mountains, buildings and towers so high
God's architecture so splendid seems
Soaring eagle swinging on the divine beams
Gracious sun lends its jewel to the rain
Envision this beauty and forget every pain

Magenta Morning

April bliss swaying in the seas
Wanton waves beckon, flaunting their moves
Dolphins dance, turtles swim
I feel joy within
The symphony that lies in the summer breeze
Euphoric nature allures the trees
Magenta morning floods the garden
Giggling silence touches the heavens
I look beyond the horizon
Release secrets to the winds
My heart is a splendid sea
Deep and flowing it'll be
Ready to endure raging rains
It may bear the harshest pains
Love is the language of my heart
Let's paint the world's canvas in this divine art

The Saucer Of Scarlet Sun

Look
The surreal sky
Sipping sorbet from the saucer of scarlet sun
Vibrant palette merging shapes and colours one by
one
Celestial radiance plays upon eyes
Gentle wind's embrace makes us alive
Rosy light mocks the night
Rubescent rays toss auburn tresses with delight
Birds' songs start new day
Crystalline euphoria spreads in ways
Trees pray and mountains crown the sky gay
Oh! look that beautiful butterfly
The spirits flying high
Winds rustle in the hair
Let's stroll with feet bare
Feel nature
Stresses cease
We find everlasting peace

Affair Of Dew Drops

Transitory
Dewdrops
Emerging
At Night
Merging
In Sunlight
~

Amaranthine
Affair

Dainty Dawn

Dainty dawn
Donned in bronze
Scribbling billet doux of eternity
Surrendering her virgin glory
To the crown of light
Auspicious aura opening doors for the new day
Sunshine piercing dark veil at the bay
Gusty hawk strolling in the sky bare
I sit in my oak rocking chair
Wondering where life desires, I would go
All I want, clocks to move slow
Feeling serenity and heavens near
Closing eyes and parting with all my fears

Vermilion Sun

Sun draped in vermilion swanking in the sky
Two hearts stitched together
Weaving tales in the eyes
Gazing at saffron dust
Sharing the celestial trust
A journey begins
On the untrodden road
Life scribbles new episodes
In nature true love born
To celebrate each blessed morn

Sighing Dusk

Stupendous sun
Reclining on mountains' couch
Withdraw radiant crown
Spread charcoal curtains in the sky
Chirping birds hide in the limbs of trees
Seagulls moving back over the sea
Sunflowers burying face in the lap of leaves
Dusk sighing, mourning the departure of light in
grief
Night, the humble mood queen adjusts her crown
Silently capturing day's throne to settle her regime

Patchwork Of Broken Hearts

Dawning of twilight arrives
Capricious hopes bloom inside
Want to lay lilies in the sky
Wish to splash pink for dusk's delight
If I find a needle and yarn of green
I'll sew flowers at the hem of trees
Fringe ocean's edges with pearls
An accessory accessible to little girls
Weave a fuchsia carpet on the plains
Stitch daisies in the lonely lanes
I'll embroider meadows in dry paths
Create the patchwork of broken hearts
Let's listen to hymns tonight
How the winds hum through trees
Opera buzzes in streams
Let's hear crickets' concert
How gracefully waves roll their skirts!
Sacred dark curls herself in dawn's chamber
Day awakes opening intoxicated eyelids from
significant slumber
Earth getting warm with sun's renewal kiss
Life - an eternal bliss

Savouring Serenity

Sandalwood scented season
Scarlet shades scattered
Sun swallowing shadows swiftly
Smooth streams shivering shyly
Stasis silence strewn
Solitary she speculates
Savouring sky's serenity

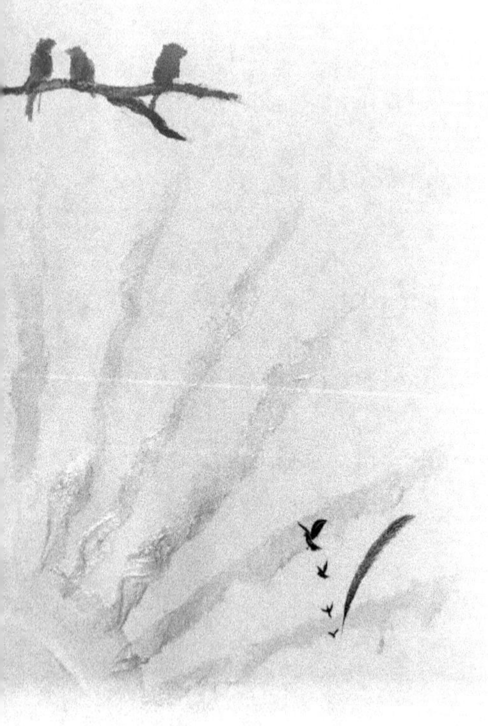

Calm sea

Calm sea revelling in silence
Reflecting sky's majestic diamonds
Glorious sun setting fire by embracing waves
Slow breeze playing melodies grave
Tiny shells drift tangled in tide
Crabs on shore moving beside
Waves' choir seducing turf
Albatross flying above the surf
As salty scent fills my soul
I cradle in the arms of water to hide
Restoring placid peace inside
I inhale life with a dip
Feel a million kisses from ocean's lips
Sit still and listen
What the waves convey
Let us be kind in every way

Winter Night

Having swept the beams of pristine sunset
Winter night wiped her brow
Began weaving tales of earth's chilly bosom
Surrendering dark whispered secrets lonesome
Dawn ready to raise his head
To toast the sanguine new page
Emerald silvery velvet in dreary December
Embroidered with inimitable gems
Slowly melting lending nectar to steady stem
Bestowing solace to jaded heart's mayhem

Nature's Tale

Day's filled with love of God
Breeze drunk with the scent of rose
Birds sucking the nectar of spring
Flowers dressed in multicolours gaily sing
Nature from earth to sky bubbling with laughter
Ripples in the rills seem like dancing little lasses
Sapphires tucked on cloud's frills
Treasure spilled on ruby hills
Wind carries pious peach
I sit on silver frosty beach
Shredding my senses
Feeling the chill in my hair
Powdered diamonds smooth my glooms bare
Relishing moments to shine my soul
Let nature tell her tale

Rendezvous With Reveries

Rain Rattling on Rooftop
Reverend Rainbow Riding on Rocks
Robins Rapping Ravishing Rhythms
Roses Rollicking Rapture Ridden
Reed Reclining on Ridge
Rhinos Rolling in Rustic Ritz
Rabbits Running
Raspberries Ripening
Rivers Rejoicing
Ripples Rock and Rolling
~

Rendezvous with Reveries

Surreal Sunflowers

Pastel hues strewn on sky's face
Wanton clouds strolling adorned in golden hem lace
Surreal sunflowers raising heads to greet the deity
sun
Tender leaves bowing gracefully in reverence
Teaching us the lessons of life
Rise, stand tall and keep the spirits high

Invincible Will

I
Rise
Bloom
Smile
Wither
Fall
~
Rise
Bloom
Smile
Wither
Fall
~
Rise
Bloom
Ouch!
Plucked
Oh!
Crushed
In dust
Cry
Sigh
Shh!
~
Little
Something
Invincible
Rising
Again

September Bliss

Leaves
Enamoured of gold
Leaving emerald
Slowly burning
Taking narrow breaths
Ready to depart
Autumn swirling in the winds
Trees' robes falling to the ground
Passions scattered in the azure skies
September bliss swaying in the eyes
How graceful is autumn!
Yet everything is falling apart
Including the ceaseless turmoil of my heart

Monarch Of The Skies

Monarch of the skies
Crown of woods
Glorify God all day
Raise branching arms to pray
New stories under it lovers weave
Birds find home in its leaves
Verdant in spring
Vibrant in summer
Emerald in rain
Gold in autumn
Ah!
I want to be a tree
Head above
Feet on field
Grow
Rise
Blossom
And never to yield

The Prince Of Rain

Bejewelled in grey
A glory cradling in the sky
Glean of roses embroider its frilly hem
The prince of rain appeared wearing cashmere
finery
Floating with the breaths of winds
Moving majestically on its swings
Over bridges, olive grooves and grape vines
I'll woo the clouds to place me on the seas benign
I'll weep rains
Mingle in the water to rise again

The June Rain

The evanescent June rain
Cuckoos sing again
Slanting showers dousing willows
Tender grass beginning to bow
Orchestra of winds
Crescendo of lightning
Thunder drums quietly
Moments later
The sun pierces the sky
Moistened earth feels so shy
Damp paths
Smiling flowers
Paper boats
Puddles flow
Peacock's dance
Rabbit's stance
Despair gone
Time keeps going on

Part- 2
Glory of Stillness

Feigned Wholeness

Pale yolk spilling from sky
Polishing my room gold
French crockery
Silver cutlery
Porcelain vase near phone
All perfectly set
Demure quiet
Wine in shelf
Cushions on couch
All maintained
And
I'm mulling by myself
Tired of feigned wholeness
Suffering from whoness

Internal Bleakness

Long lazy languid day
Sombre twilight crept in
Melancholy dances more vehemently
Shadows deepening internal bleakness
Pale starlit dark
Moon drenched pathways
Hills tasselling the rim of skies
Splendid silhouette of pointed spruce
And I'm inebriated by the bountiful betrayal of him

Tangerine Crown

Stoic silence
No one in sight
Just lingering quiet
A shadow moves
Fireflies aglow
Wind starts the show
Choir begins
Leaves rustle
Bees hum
Birds chirp
Crickets sing
Temple bells ring
Here comes the king in tangerine crown
In veneration of ethereal music
Dark elopes in grey gown

Sleepless Nights And Bootless Cries

Sleepless nights
I go to the terrace
Smell the fragrance of silence
See the silhouetted trees
Listen to the humming insects
Look at the neon light on cobblestone and my
shadows
Throat needs to be quenched
I drink darkness
With withered lips and desolate eyes
~

Moments of bootless cries

Old Stories

Moonlight scribbling sonnets in silver calligraphy
I leaned back to take a long sip of thoughts
Doleful drizzles
Smell of moss
Old stories reviving in
The confinement of heart
Nostalgia brewing
In the stained teapot
Crestfallen enjoyment of the rhythms of
Drip
Drop
Drip
Drop

Melancholy – My Companion

Lavender sky tossing the silvery ice
Hills adorned in chiffon white
Pines draped in sizzling snow
Pristine earth dazzled in ice-kissed glow
Wanton winter peered through glass
I closed the windows
Pulled the curtains fast
Invited melancholy
To share my pain
Memories flowed like summer rain

Another Aimless Day

Sun rises
New day
New expectations
I put my mask on again
The one
That I hung on the peg
Behind the door last night
Long grey roads
Harmonizing with my thoughts
Just moving on endlessly
Waiting for the destination
How we know
Some things exist
Just for existence
I walk
~

Another aimless day

Awkward Hush

Indian summer
Total stillness
Sitting at the terrace
In the deadly dark
Lonely roads
Awkward hush
Shattered by cricket's song
Thoughts like tumbleweed
Whirling along
Explaining to myself
Where I am
Where I belong
Unknown pathways
A stranger in my own home
~

Forlorn

Glory Of Stillness

Walking alone on sandy carpet of beach
Around me are the rhythms of silence
Beyond me are the melodies of waves
Kaleidoscope of wrong turns moving inside
Each grain of sand
Curing me of myself
Closing my eyes
Unbuttoning my heart
To feel the glory of stillness

Searching My Existence

My endeavour to find
what is what
Who is who
Left me fractured and nonessential
I want to hide
In a poet's words
In a painter's art piece
In a philosopher's thought
Dissolving in fathoming
The depth of my existence

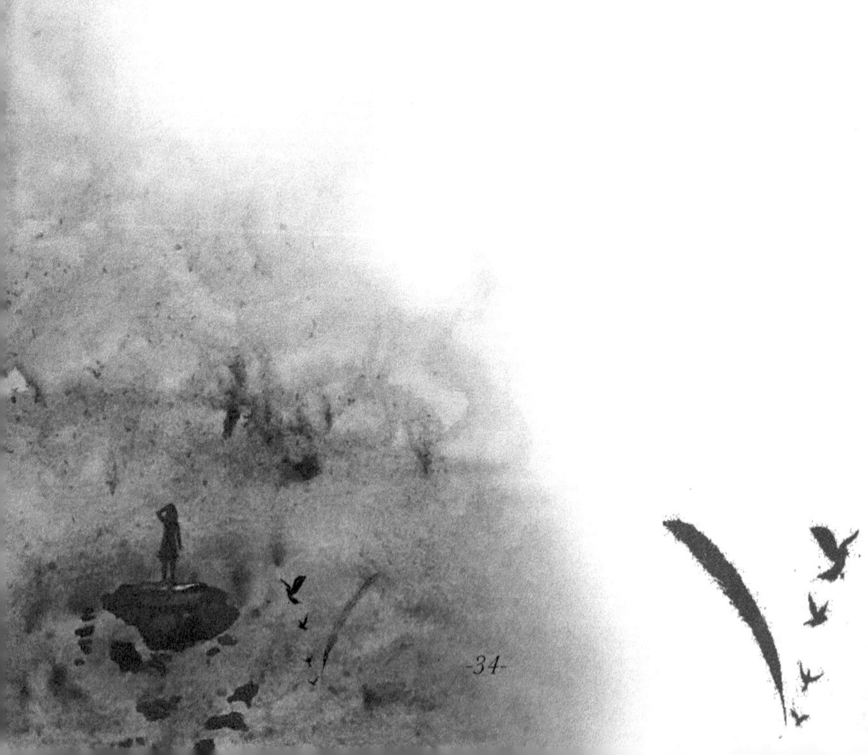

Peerless Silence

2:15 am
Sitting alone
Peerless silence
Solemn stillness
Sipping storm in chalice
Feverish lamplight
I wish I could write
Tacenda thesaurus brewing inside
A drop to fall in lucid disquiet
Tears wither
Veins shiver
Music of hiccups
Hollow passions whisper
O obstinate dawn!
Don't intrude
I'm relishing sombre obscurity
Velvet darkness gives me security
Shhh!
Celebrating loneliness

Midnight Anxiety

Silent streets
Columns of thoughts
In increasing hollow hours
l embellished my scornful scars
Then, I took a bite of moon
Drank the sorbet of stars
Ready to sleep in the arms of dark
While listening to the lullabies
Of silence in winter night
~

Midnight Anxiety

My Suave Loneliness

Creakkk

Something broke
Or the void inside
Playing symphonies
With stillness
Dark night
Insects' murmurs
Under downlight
Breaking the terrible silence
How static
How empty
No desires
No thoughts
No fears
Just
Me and
My suave loneliness
~
Hush!

Peculiar Sighs

Silence staring at the face of darkness
Sobs echoing in long rainy night
Wounds flamed by vehicle's garish light
Watery eyes
Peculiar sighs
Tattooed thighs
And lonesome me
Invited memories to a ambrosial soiree
Opened my treasure box
Withered roses fell off
A pretty shell
Pale letters
Satin scarf
A few torn photographs
And some moments
Where he scattered like time
Ticking in my each second
Memories hung up longer than invited
May the sunrays never pour
I want obscurity
In this dead hour

Orchestra Of My Pain

Trumpet and trombone
Flutes and saxophone
Neon lights and dance rhythms
Tequila and salt of skins
Friday hopes
Time to mask off
Calypso music
Expressing the inexpressible
Chorus melodies
Telling tales insane
Synchronising with the orchestra of my pain

Sacred Hours

Sweltering scarlet stream
Flowing in veins
Still freezing cold reigning inside
An unusual lifelessness
Has something broken ?
Or the listless silence speaking
A lump is blocking the throat
Loneliness clenching pores
Oh!
Unearthly dark
You cover my scars
Long live sacred hours!

My Sun Carries Dark

Cultivating loneliness
Allowing my soul to grow
Rhythms of silence creep in
When the world is hushed
My sun carries darkness in its womb
Have to stop finding empathetic people
Who fear to invade my dark inside
Telling you, dear man
My inside and outside don't match
But
I'm me

Mysterious Nothingness

My apathetic shadows to the ceiling
Dancing dilatory to the quivering flames
The mind so contemplative
With some scarlet theme
Wore most beautiful lie
Where sabotaged smile gleams
The taste of deepest scars
In desolate regime
Ah!
I love
Familiar darkness
Lazy bleakness
Mysterious nothingness
Bolting all doors to listen to sentient silence

I'm a boat

A dusky solitary evening
Sitting at the bank of river
Watching boats
It speaks
It bears
Tears the heart of water
Tossed by winds and waves
Scribble gloom
When shores swallow its edges
I, too
Am a boat
Worn out
Dejected
Rejected
Giving up strife
Gurgling down, 0 life!
~
Who understands?

Savvy Hurt

Dark clouds looming over me
Waiting for the rain to burst
I'll sit under downpour for hours
Wash away his smell from my pores
To sink the savvy hurt
Gnawing at my delicate core
Watch floral shine growing fast
From the million glittery pieces of my battered heart

Part - 3

Where Clouds Cradle Dreams

Walk with me
Where willows weep
Cedars bend with age
Web your fingers through mine
And trap stories of youth
We'll talk of buttermilk noon
And relish it with chapatti of moon
Can you take me
Where clouds cradle dreams?
We'll stroll in the milky way
And sip nectar of the North Star's beams
We'll lie face to face on the crescent
I'll spread desires beneath you
And weave stories fluorescent
Speak softly
I'm the best thing that happened to you
Whisper my name
Love me with closed eyes
I'll steal your fragrance
To save in my pockets
Your scent is the periapt of my life

Ambrosial Syrup

Place
Your hands on me
Bow a bit
To taste the ambrosial syrup of my lips
Close your eyes
Reach beyond reality
And, think of me
As wine in a feast
You have been dying to drink
Each day
Each hour
Each minute

Take Me Away

Take me away
To the unknown
Where moonlight fills me with fire
Where I can
Undress my reasons
Unfold my yearnings
Draw me close
Thinking that doomsday is near
Hold me
As if it's the last night
Embrace me
Raging storms are approaching
Kiss me
Until I die
Love me
Let me take last hiccup in your chest
There I'll find my eternal peace and rest
~

Ultimate Emancipation

A Night With Him

A million galaxies are exploding inside
Rainbows melt in my mouth
The scent of moonflower emanates from each pore
Saint in me losing all reasons from the core
My spirits spreading the wings of peafowl
Heartbeats echoing the universe in prowl
Goosebumps playing the electrifying rhythms of
storms
Peachy blue dawn driving me insane
What a feeling of immortal longings sweet!
Stars and planets are spread beneath my feet
Just
A
Night
With
Him

Let Me Love Thee

Clock struck nine
Light succumbs to darkness
Melancholy broods
No zephyr so far
Daylilies fold themselves
Fickle stars slide to their place
I close all doors
Hold spirits tight
Come, my love
Leave thy art
Just one kiss then silently part
Come, see me only
For last time
Weep, my love, weep
Let me love thee
Till I stop to breathe
Time will stand still
Between your lips and mine
I'll live in those moments for lifetime

Forbidden Fruit

Little cottage
Besieged with snow
Without him
My pulse beats low
Ah! dear
Cool the singed object
With feisty fingertips
Ignite my passion
With Rosebud lips
Prolong, O elysian snow! Prolong
Extend thy frigid reign
Let me taste the forbidden fruit
And bequeath my Eden in his name

Polka Dot Night

Twilight kissing the sun goodbye
To embrace the silver polka dot night
Sensual tones of darkness unnerving naked silence
My heart skipped a beat when your hazel eyes
glistened like diamonds
Take me to a carpet of daisies
Where stars dangle a bit low
To match your radiance
Sit under the maple
Tuck a rose in my hair and
Touch my edges with poems
Oh! Hold that tiny bead of sweet sweat on your
fingertips sliding down my collarbone
Hold me like a lute and play with its strings till dawn
I'll watch you breathless lying in my arms

Tale Of His Eyes

Brighter than shimmering stars
Carry softness of a million flowers
Oceans flow, storms glow
Yet so calm
Mysteriously searching unknown
Poets compose
Lovers explore
Miracles hang in space
Angels too feel the ache
Tale of his eyes
Where I find rhythms of my life

Breathless

Love me now
Love me here
Draw me close
Hold me like beer
Love me in peace
Love me in chaos
I have only you
In my thoughts
Love me at dawn
Love me at dusk
Love my soul
Leave aside lust
Love my smile
Love my pain
Love me completely
Beyond loss or gain

Huh!
Breathless

Fifty Shades Of Pink

Evening frost bewitching the night
Earth in diaphanous chiffon alluring moonlight
I found myself
Obsessed with his elfin face
Turquoise eyes
Brown curl, licking his forehead ~
A Sultry touch
That gave me fifty shades of pink
Pushed all inhibitions aside under pillow
Threw all fears to the stars
I reclined in his arms
Untied my hair to fall on his chest
Senses commenced its journey
To find its sanctum at sin's behest
Dedicated to him
My sleep
My heart
My moments
My self
~
Night turned into celebration

Make Me Magnificent

When I first met you
I felt I'd known you since ages
Shared secrets
That I didn't ever want
Come, let me taste your scent
Touch me and make me magnificent
Sit with me, love
Tell me, you like the sound of my name
Say, you desire my breath on your skin
Lay me down gently
Kiss me on forehead
And, murmur "You are Beautiful "
I want to make you happy
I'll drink all your tears
And dance like a whore
I'll lasso the moon for you
Then make a home between my ribcage
Live there
Till my bones crush
Just promise to love me
When I'll no longer be new

Moments Of Euphoric Bliss

Waiting for hours
For the moments
The moments of euphoric bliss
You came
Raw and unmasked
With dark composite smile
And intoxicating eyes
With an orchard of love letters
Enough for me to fall in love
You invaded my every breath
I ~ bared and scared
Waiting to be consumed
Tingling sensation of
Night exotic
Vibes erotic
Ah! Pull me
Lift me
Win me
Move like life
In my veins
To be mine
In all ways
Always

Fatal Egos

He came
Kissed my forehead
His fingers brushed my hair
Stunned to silence not by his gestures
But by the languor in his hands
My chest ached
It's a burden
I was glad to carry again
He moved dumbly
I wanted to hold him
To say unsaid
To cry in his chest
~

He's gone
~

Fatal Egos

I Want To Touch You

O man of umber eyes and dimpled chin
I want to touch you
When you are asleep
I'll perch your head in my lap
And tuck that brown curl back
Laying down on your forehead
I want to play with your knuckles
And devour your earlobe
Hold me
I feel safe in your embrace
Give me space, just a little
In the corner of your heart
Let me move further
In that enlightened area
Say my name
And let me hear if it echoes inside
Give me a glance
Look into the storms in my eyes
Feel how my heart sighs
You are the weakness that makes me strong

A Glass Of Poetry

London streets
Winter rains
Tiny drops
Knocking windowpane
I whisper
While holding his hands
Read me a book
Paint my toenails
Braid jasmines in my plaits
Sing love Songs
Dangle in my arms
Drive me insane
Caress my every inch
With thirsty lips
Hug me tight
Kiss me long
O dear!
Pour me a glass of poetry
I want to get drunk
And Sleep

Another Chance

Languor hour
Wore gossamer gown
The pink one
Wet strands dampening revealing curve
Sanctuary blossoming on face
Roses on lips grew
Where divinity too bowed
Bonnie bosom like strawberry bed
Yearning to spend a few moments in his chest
She stuffed smiles in her pockets
Gathered courage in her hands
Snatched moon from the night
Squeezed it in his cup
'Savour for last time,' she said
Knelt before him
Traced his firm jawline
A bead trickled from his temple
She sucked that with lust
Began playing harmonica on his chest
Composed a concerto of pulsating heartbeats
And, whispered in destiny's ears
"May you lend us another chance to begin again" ?

Undress Me

Kiss me with wet nib
Moisten my dry pages
Light my dark heart with ink
I offer you
My each breath
Undress me
Word by word
I'll remain
Bare till death

Be My Forever

Meet me under twilight skies
Where winds toss our tresses
We'll watch sunset of peach rays
Honeysuckle breeze will cool our faces
Butterflies kiss the rose
We'll sit barefoot beneath sycamore
Birds' song diffuses greys however
In this ever changing world
Be my forever

Come Inside, Love

Breeze in my love, unhesitatingly, like cool winds
Enter my courtyard
Like a sparrow invades my balcony
Look, the rain has moistened the grass for your
arrival
Wind carries the fragrance of roses
Don't press the doorbell
I feel your vibes
I know your scent
Come inside
I've spread the evening for you
Tucked smiles in pathways
I've stirred my love in your tea
Move in
Bring some subtle moments
A few memories
And
When you depart
Take some part of me
And
Leave something of you with me

Grow Old With Me

There is no other you
Only you
Though I skip my breaths and my heart beats high
But I need you to remain alive
I feel
So organic
So platonic
So exquisite
Without demonstrations
Without inhibitions
Bloom in blossoming an orchid with you
You are my enchanted dawn
My dusk's calm
Lie with me for hours
Let me coil in the safety of your arms
Touch me with words
Tell me your favourite songs
Tell me which book you read before sleeping
Tell me when I come across your thoughts
Tell me you need me
Make all your fears obviously known
I feel more for you than I have shown
~

My love
Grow Old With Me

Part - 4
Lilac Shades of Life

Being Benign

Dare to dream
Bind these dreams with sunlight
Touch planets and stars
Awake in the universe with spirits high
Let galaxies melt
In your rainbow desires
Just learn to smile
Smash fears of self
Be a better version of yourself
Grow wings to fly high
Rise, O gracious soul!
Keep magic alive in your eyes
Let's scribble 'love' across the sky
Whisper, 'Life is beautiful'
Make your existence worthwhile
Dance in rain
Sing from soul
Burn egos like fireflies
Grow kindness and Shine
Wipe tears of others
By being benign

A Conversation Between Earth & Sky

Today
Again
Earth asked sky,
"Why have you tears in your eyes?
Susurrus of clouds sighing in your sight"
Falling drops touched earth and whispered,
"You too have deadly oceans in your eyes
With anxiety in mellow smiles,
You just endure
And
I simply outpour"

Contemplating Life

Sitting on a boulder in the middle of stream
Contemplating life in moments of peace
Water playing games in-between my toes
Lyrical chants of winds calm my soul
Velvety grass sways
Waves enjoy their play
I close my eyes
As the breeze caresses my face
Let me fade in nature's holy embrace

The Fabric Of Humanity

Spend life in weaving a quilt of life
Sewing brokenness with the yarn of strife
Darning ripped relations with needle of desires
Doing the patchwork of illusions dire
Her time is so designed
Find peace in hobbies refine
Knotting
Knitting
Stitching
A tapestry so divine
The fabric of humanity will shine

Paper Boats And Dolls

Cherubic eyes
Celestial smiles
Running with clouds and counting stars
Playing with rabbits for endless hours
That scent of a pencil's shavings
Struggles with commas and theorems
Ah! Life of paper boats and dolls
Marbles, puddles and fairy's calls
O Lord!
Take away my youth
Rekindle in me the child of truth

Hold Me Like A Poem

Ah! Man
Nothing but a peerless desire
Just love me like a poet
Make me thy book
You want to read
Every day
Each moment
Wrap me around its pages
I'll hide between spaces
Breathe in letters
Create lines of emotions
Dear man,
Let me savour thy sapphire potion
Hold me like a poem
I want to feel alive
And peacefully die
In your ink

A Leaf About To Fall

Purple veins and shadows of time
Wrinkles exhibit his story sublime
Sealed lips depict the pain
Wise parenting seems to be in vain
Prays for patience and friends a few
What a masquerade of smiles blue
Time trips
Spoon drops
Pants wet
Tears flow

A withered leaf is about to fall

That Candy Shop

O life
Touch me
Like dawn kisses dark goodbye
And paint me in hues of vibrant sighs
Hold me
Until twilight spreads ebony
I know
Pain is a part of destiny
Take me back to that candy shop
I miss smeared faces even more
It's okay to get silly
Laugh and dance
We never get a second chance

Oh! Mamma

Night cast a black spell of dark
Stars shone brilliantly at that hour
I sat in the open
To savour this glorious silence
Felt a bright star calling my name
I swayed my head
Held my breath
My heart skipped
A tear slipped
Oh mamma!
Come
Call me your baby
Take me in your lap
For one last time
Please Mamma!

Becoming Poetry

Can I be
A drop of ink
Falling
~
Reaching on his paper
~
Becoming Poetry

Pour Thy Pain

WRITERS~
Papers are pale
Take my skin
As parchment

Pens are subtle
Take my bones
To express the complex

Need indelible flow of ink
My veins are oozing blues
~
Now, pour thy pain
Let the chimneys blaze
And cups overflow with wine
Weave truth in words
And sing melodies divine
Wrap thyself around pages
Where epochs speak
Breathe kindness between lines
This World needs peace
Let writings show stoutest of hopes in view
O Writer!
Paint 'Today' in the brightest hues

Seasons Come And Go

She wore a black brocade gown
Held red carnations with white daffodils
Placed them on the stairs
Where they used to sit
Shed few tears
To bid adieu to a phantasm
Turned back on the way
Where seasons come and go
Paving the path for new
~
She embraced herself
And
Spring came earlier

Her Grace Lies In Wrinkles

Brick-red lips
A purple strand highlights the greys
Pointed stilettos
Velvet gown
Smiles are her crown
Enjoys the life
The charming lass
A little badass
Eyes twinkle
Her grace lies in her wrinkles
In lonely night
She weaves a string of memories
Lasso moon to spend night with

Honour The Woman

Honour the woman
For the fire in her soul
She fights frantic battles
Broken but appears whole
Honour her
For the tides of her love
She may be fierce
She isn't always your dove
Honour her
Don't pull her down
She is the maker of generations
Wears her humility like crown

To Be Or Not To Be

Bare sentiments
Sadness stirring
'Drinking Alone in the Moonlight'
Suffering the pangs of 'Hamlet
To be or not to be
What 'If'
I delve into "The Road Not Taken' deliberately
Oh! life
'How do I love thee'
Stay for a while
Moments are slipping
Stay
Oh! life..

How Arcane Are Poets

How arcane are poets
For making butterflies of words
Sucking lavender hearts benign
Loving them feels like sonnet playing a mandolin
along the curve of spine
They smell like ambers and aromatic oils
Their poems slather balm of bizarre void
Poets-benevolent despots
Flirt
Feign
But
They beautify the pain

You Are The Best

Love thyself
Radiate the purity of your soul
Flaunt your enchanted self beyond control
Shed, what weighs you down
Don't try to fit in
You are born to stand out
Stop raping your thoughts
At the opinion of others
Raise your head and tell yourself
"YOU ARE THE BEST,
SOMETHING INCREDIBLE"

War And Whizzing Life

Earth draped in tattered scarlet
Crimson clouds shedding tears
Gentlemen playing poker
Ladies giggling in parties
Army battling
Crows cawing
God is laughing
Life is whizzing

And I'm painting my nails red

Life Is Blissful

Midnight
Moon hung up high
To greet the night
Birds in their nests
Flowers too taking rest
Time of stillness
Moments of introspection
I stared out of window
To restore my spirits
A firefly winked
Denounced the dark
Hopes minced
So calm the hour
Nothing to miss
Life is a bliss

Vain Verses Plain

Playing poker in high key
Feigned show-off lurking in psyche
Chatting useless, misled
Leave the children half fed
Parties cheesy
How busy!
~

Living in a cottage
Soothing silence
Basil at door
Working all day without getting bored
Humming with bees
Children upon knees
Life at ease!

Part- 5
Musings Of My Soul

She is Aurora

She carries blues in her scarlet heart
Face depicts melting hues of discordant thoughts
Pale desires crop from indigo dreams
Tears flow with smiles like a gentle stream
She speaks softly like ringing of temple bells
Exhales kindness as if it's her religion
Doesn't go on pilgrimages
But pacifies the crying children
Possesses vintage heart away from feigned craft
She is Aurora, armoured with squashed colours
Painting her tomorrows in dust and ashes

My Orphan Soul

Peep in
Come
I'm unfolding my layers for you
Stripping my laces, my precious jewels
Peeling my tan skin
Go deep, man
Tear my veins
Move
Break my ribcage
There, in the depth
Something red is quivering
No, not here
Move forward
Invade my unexplored region
There lies my purity
My orphan soul

Love this

An Insane In Sane World

Whooshing noise of untold stories
Piercing mesmerizing silence
Words wringing the tears of my heart
To fall as diamonds
This gives me strength
I become character l want to be
I do what I feel
I explore what I'm afraid of
Writing makes me~ Me
An insane in sane world
l am not merely a name
Or an object of your tangled play
But, A woman
With a fortitudinous heart
That feels and deserves love~
An exquisite brain
Of intangible tolerance
That understands and knows
Wrong and right

My silence is my choice
Respect that

Museum Of Memories

Falling apart
In bits and parts
Wandering in museum of memories
In the haze of scars
Scarlet dreams clutter in the crippled birches
Scent of gloom everywhere perches
Something is breaking inside
But tired of mending
Is it a parade of bleakness?
I own you, low
Now, it's your turn to bow

I Deserve To Be- Me

I want to be Nobody
At barren wasteland
The weight of belonging
Is too heavy
~
I
Deserve
To
Be
Me
~
Free from expectations

Masquerade Of Brokenness

How skilfully
She is spreading her pain
In the form of bonita butterflies
Penetrating deep her feigned smiles
Blank eyes whispering excruciating sighs
Unable to understand life's games
Never wants to win
Loses each turn willingly without shame
For every dead desire
She cocoons a piece of her heart
Inserts that, right near her feet, under her skin
Her steps start composing rattling rhythms
~

The Masquerade of brokenness

There Once Lived A Girl

There once lived a girl
Who licked from sky the lollipop moon
Rode hopes where sun spreads caramelized noon
Filled her eyes with poems that grew of tarnished
desires
On icy heart, she spilled fire
Giggled like trickle of stardust yet broken
What a fool she was
Dreamt with eyes wide open
She was skilled in music and dance
And the old art of romance
She liked queer things
Humility she poured
Smiles with panic tinged
She spoke gentle and kind
The pure soul so blind
Alas!
Caged for her life
She forgot
Queens should be cold and wise

I'm A Dandelion Pip

Sometimes
I feel
I'm a dandelion pip
A pale patch
On the emerald dress
Stubbornly alive
Growing without
Any aim in life
I fly
Where winds desire
I'm on a journey with time
Since east is dropping crimson fire
I move on
It's my serendipity to move
Uprooted
Blown away
Scattered
To rise again

She Is Not An Angel

She
A beautiful dawn
Or a dancing fawn
A moonlit night
Or a zephyr delight
Carrying seashells
A voice like ringing bells
Making castles in the sand
Applying henna on her hands
She's hedonist and ascetic entwined
Her thoughts are the ultimate shrine
Finds comfort in chaos
Loves beyond gain or loss
Grows asphalt flowers from ashes
Oceans flow forever under her lashes
Caged in expectations
She grows wings of wilderness
Casts spell with her eyes
Spends hours at the seaside
Bites senses in appetite
Smokes desires at midnight
Inhales toxic fumes of sighs
Wants to drink sometimes and die
She is not an angel
She sometimes lies
Putting on mask she smiles then cries
So silent
So raw

So naive
Falls in love
And
Forgets to smile
In the wait of right time
She dies in her own lifetime

I'm Lotus

Who has spilled the golden gems
In the murky water
These palest amethysts
Basking dreamily in serenity
Purging my soul adroitly
From the muck and mire it arises
Holding in heart, the beauty of sunrise
Write divine lyrics on water like poetess
From the muddy suffering
I too have become Lotus

Forbidden Romance

On a salty coast
Sun painting my skin into a golden tan
Leaving nostalgic silage of wet sand
Waves kissing the shores in nude lip-gloss
Sky savouring clouds' candyfloss
I pick myself up
Step into the sea
Forget all
Mind is free
Desires dance
Rekindling a forbidden romance

A Million Moods

One moment
A million moods
I dance at the tune of life's lute
I lean in thoughts
I laugh loudly at silly jokes
I cry when I listen to sad songs
I weep then wipe nose
Stumble wearing stilettos
I've crack in my heels
I kneel, I feel, I heal
I shed tears when I laugh
I spill drinks
I trip
I slip
Lost and forgotten me
A little awkward me
But real me

Satins And Frilly Laces

Neither have wisdom nor style
But I can offer you my seclusion and velvety skies
No satins or frilly laces befall
To present my love with all
Only a heart enlightened and kind
With an honest mind
No favours I demand
Just be with me in every dusk and dawn

Beautifully Chaotic

She is alpha
Heroine of her life
Though it wasn't in the script
Beautifully chaotic
Finding fullness in fragility
Devouring antique darkness
Bathing in moonbeams
Dancing amidst wolves
Singing with winds
Tying anklets of clouds
Braiding wildflowers in plaits
And
Then he comes

I'm Caged In My Body

I'm caged in my body
Yearn to fly high
To unknown heights
Bird inside
Fluttering its wings
Struggling for release
From stubborn hinges
Dark abyss
Digging depths
Unable to be free
Falling mercilessly
Holding onto breaths
O skies!
Extend your arms
Let me slumber
Oblivious of subtle harm

She's Magic

She's a divine aura incarnate
Hides in herself galaxies great
Adept at gathering the shards of her heart
Transforms them into stars
Scatters them into night sky
In her soul stardust lies
Wearing wildflowers
Wine ferments in her eyes
Roses grow on her lips
Sanctuary blossoms in smiles
Loves weaving poems
Dances during midnight cravings
Builds a universe of words
Laughs loudly
You may call her absurd
Enjoying the little things in life
Free from all strife
Kindness she sows
Where angels too bow
She's magic
She's deep
She's logic
A dream to keep
She's kind
A poem benign

A Fragile Wall

I'm
A fragile wall
Painted with terracotta
Moistened with moss
Supposed to stand still
When all is trying to hit
No one looks at my plight
Tears fall fast at night
Self-consuming my grief
Tale is not so brief
Invite my naked soul
Unwrap my swaddle whole
Ready to break free
To fly free

Waiting For Footprints

Winter knocked softly
Sitting near window
Looking at the unpaved white chiffon path
Waiting for footprints
No one but abundant memories arrive
He won't come, I realized
Turned to mirror
To see grey hair and fine lines
Ah!
The only hero I need
Is standing tall
In the looking glass

Where Am I Wrong?

Where am I wrong?
Peeled my skin
Pierced my pores
Tore my silly heart
To seek acceptance
To get love without hurt
Did I expect more?
Midnight dark sighs
To hear my cries
Solitude shivers
Heart quivering
No one near
Nothing I need
Royal silence
Still paying heed
Break my bones
Grind them
Spread them in dust

NIRVANA!

Breaking Free

Cosmos lies within me
I'm made of star stuff
Midnights fascinate me
My hollow heart delves in crazy bleakness
Ah life!
Offer me more dark
I know
How to turn
Pain in planets
Gloom in galaxies
Malice in moonlight
Another me evolves
I'm more than I am
Shattering my orbits
Soaring beyond spaces
Running amok among stars
Breaking free for breakthroughs
~
Dare You!

Author's Bio

Despite trained as an educator, Monica preferred to be a home maker by day and a writer by night. Born and brought up in India, Monica got master's degree in English Literature. She worked as a head of an educational institution. But chose the road less travelled by, by dedicating her full time to family life after marriage. Monica took refuge in words from mundane life and began writing her debut poetry book 'A New Dawn Of A Hundred Hues' after getting inspired by her friends of Twitter. Her spare time spent in contemplating life with sips of ginger cinnamon tea.

To know more about Monica ,kindly keep in touch via web:

Website- www.poetichues.in

Twitter- Monica B @_Being_Benign

Instagram- Monica B @_being_benign